# Self

## A Guide to Self-Actualization

COLE FELDMAN

*Self: A Guide to Self-Actualization*
By Cole Feldman

www.colejfeldman.com

ISBN 978-0-9963608-0-7
Published by Cole Feldman

Disclaimer: This book details the author's personal opinions. The author is not a licensed professional and is not engaged to render any type of professional advice. The author and publisher do not assume and hereby disclaim any liability to any party for any loss or damage, caused by errors or omissions as a result of negligence, accident, or any other cause. This is a comprehensive limitation of liability that applies to all damages, including (without limitation) compensatory; direct, indirect or consequential; loss of income or profit; loss of or damage to property and claims of third parties. In addition, the author and publisher do not represent or warrant that the information accessible via this book is accurate, complete or current.

*For the amusement of my less anxious self*

*"Focused ability motivated by need brings intangible thought to physical reality so that we might actualize our selves before death"*

# CONTENTS

# INTRODUCTION

She had soft pouty lips. He watched them move and felt his pick up where hers left off, coaxing hers to dance again. They watched through the window as Chicago passed by in the night.

He did not make the mistake of rationalizing, as he usually did, the emotions involved in such encounters—human relationships and the laws of attraction that govern them.

They stayed up most the night talking, melting into the hardwood floor of his empty apartment bedroom. She appealed deeply to his nature, forced his humanity to overwhelm his mind.

Together, the capacities of their hearts were far greater than any thoughts their minds might have otherwise produced, so, like a pair of rational economic actors, they loved, because the opportunity cost was far too great to do anything else.

For two summer nights, she made him forget about everything else in the world. Then she was gone.

❖❖❖

She is less one person than she is many people, oftentimes not even a person at all. She is home. She is whoever, or whatever, makes me forget that we are finite; and she does so, ironically, by appealing to those parts of me that are most human.

It was after she left, when I sat alone in the basement unit of an apartment building in the north suburbs of Chicago, that I began to write; only then, I was not writing to create a book.

I returned to college for my sophomore year, but I did not stop writing; in fact, I often wrote instead of paying attention in class. I wrote just to write, to clear my head of thoughts, until I had written too much to remain unbound, lest I lose track of it all.

As I filled this book with what I had become, it began to consume everything I once was. Graduating with honors, working for a top firm, and all else that had previously been my identity became irrelevant. It was more important that I filled this book—that might live forever—with ideas I might have otherwise forgotten.

❖❖❖

The only idea from this book that you mustn't forget is the very same one that you were already most likely to remember even before having started to read; it is simple: we will die.

That is rather blunt, I suppose, but bluntness allows this book to be so short, and, being a believer in brevity, I will not be subtle.

From the sole assumption of death, I will make an argument for self-actualization. We are finite; therefore we must seek to become all that we can before dying.

This book teaches you to self-actualize, bringing to physical reality your intangible thoughts, by a particular process: first knowing yourself, then harnessing the motivation of your needs and exercising your focused abilities. We repeat this process until we die, as the sum of all that we have done, as all that we could have been.

This book will surely teach you to possess all that you desire, to become wealthy and realize your wildest dreams, but it is also much more than that, because what is any of this worth after we die?

This book teaches you *how* to become your best self, but differs from other self-help books in that it will also continually ask the question: *why* must we become our best selves?

This is philosophy in the Socratic sense combined with a more modern self-help book, examining *how* we should live through the lens of *why* we should live in the first place.

The knowledge within this book comes from a glimpse through one man, no more or less human than anyone else, to the governing dynamics of the whole race. At our cores, we have much in common; we are all the same species, born to live and die, so *why not* live to become all that we can? This is our story, of great potential and actualization—the story of the human self.

# SELF-ACTUALIZATION

*TO BE ALL THAT WE CAN*

We will begin with a question that is simple enough: Why is there something rather than nothing? As a creature simultaneously under the conditions of both thought and existence, I often ask myself, "Why do we exist rather than not exist? Why do I exist?"

I have wondered most of my short life about the answers to these questions. I am still young; I suppose my restlessness may be the result of having not yet stumbled upon those truths that allow my elders to be so calm and well mannered.

For nineteen years, I looked outward for answers—to religion, then philosophy, and finally, but only briefly, to science, intermittently distracted from the search by my humans needs.

Philosophy says we should seek truth. Religion says God is Truth. Science says we should be rational. Hedonism says we should get drunk. Capitalism says we should get rich.

I lived according to all of this but was still certain of nothing and even began to feel conflicted as I learned of contradictions between ideologies that were previously in accord with my reason.

I knew that if two ideologies contradicted one another, then both could not be true—this is the law of non-contradiction. For example, if a theist claims God does exist and an atheist claims God does not exist, they cannot both be telling the truth.

The uncertainty and conflict only worsened as I learned. Each new ideology unveiled a contradiction with a known ideology. A capitalist behaves differently than a Catholic and a utilitarian behaves differently than Kant; so I was left uncertain of how to act.

Given the vast number of ideologies that man has invented and their inevitable contradictions with one another, though many may hold pieces of the truth, it is probable that the great majority of our belief systems are false, at least in part.

If truth were subjective, then there would be many true religions, philosophies, and other ideologies, which would stand to make all this a great deal easier; yet, it is not, because to say, "Truth is subjective," is itself an objective claim, and therefore self-refuting.

I have accepted now that I cannot know with certainty which ideology is the truth. In my whole life, even if spending just a few moments on each ideology, I would not have the time to consider every single ideology that any man has ever held to be true.

Whatever exists beyond our natural realm, or even what exists here, hidden within microbial cell walls, or out there, at the outer bounds of the expansive universe, may very well affect how we might presently live, but religion and philosophy and science cannot seem to agree, and I am not wise enough to know myself.

After nineteen years of wondering, there were only two things of which I had become relatively certain: First, as Socrates taught me, I knew that I knew nothing, at least not with absolute certainty. And second, of all the things about which I was uncertain, I was least uncertain—or, most certain—that I would die.

Then, and only recently, did I look inward, into myself, and alas, I found something there. Not an answer, but a crutch, at least, on which we might rest our injured beliefs for a short while. A guide for what we might do in the meantime as we continue to search for answers that we may never find, for our behavior amidst uncertainty.

It is about this crutch that this book is written, having born in me more peace, satisfaction, and contentment than the combination of all temporary pleasures masquerading as happiness.

It is self-actualization: to be all that we can be, to actualize our greatest potential selves.

### Decision under uncertainty: an argument from death.

It is conceivable that there is no meaning for the life of man, that our species is purposeless, that there is no reason that we exist rather than not exist, that nothing matters—this, I imagine, is the worst possibility for man, to be purposeless. It is my greatest fear.

The real tragedy is that there is no way of knowing for sure—as is the case with anything, I suppose—but decision theory offers a temporary solution: because there exists the possibility of consequences from each individual human life, eternal consequences even, we must each then behave as if eternal consequences will certainly result from our individual finite existences.

Because my fear that nothing matters is rational but not certain, it would certainly be irrational for me to live as if nothing matters; because it is possible that there is much at stake, infinite gain or loss, both for others and myself.

(1) If man lives to be less than he could have potentially been and his life has eternal consequences, then infinite loss is suffered as the difference between his lesser self and fully actualized self.

(2) If man lives to be less than he could have potentially been and his life does *not* have eternal consequences, then he gains finite pleasures otherwise sacrificed to work toward self-actualization.

(3) If man becomes all that he can and his life has eternal consequences, then infinite gain is won as the difference between his fully actualized self and his lesser self.

(4) If man becomes all that he can and his life does *not* have eternal consequences, then he loses the finite pleasures he sacrificed to work toward self-actualization.

This assumes what is to be contributed by man is not negligible on an infinite scale. The logic of this argument is similar to Pascal's Wager. The general conclusion is this: a rational man seeking to maximize gain and minimize loss for both others and himself chooses to live to become self-actualized.

If man lives to be less than he could have potentially been, he and all those who would have benefitted from his work, both during his life and after his death by the butterfly effect, suffer loss. If man is self-actualized, he gains for himself and many others.

We can act as if life does not matter in death. We can lie in the ground and relax for eternity. But we only have this life to be all that we can. The rest of existence is likely out of our control.

We are god-like creative minds at the helms of able human bodies motivated by human need, yet we are still mortal, able to do only so much before we die, so we must live now, while we still can.

*Why we must make a decision under uncertainty.*

Imagine if an author sat down at his desk to write a book, but first said to himself, "I will not touch my pen to the paper until I am absolutely certain of *why* I am writing." What would happen?

He would never write a single letter. He would sit there for a long while: considering the nature of writing itself, then the elements of language, even the purpose of communication. He might never even consider reading a book by another author, so consumed in his own mind with first answering the question of *why*.

But even if he were to sit and think for his whole life about *why* he should write, he could never know with absolutely certainty, because he is human, and therefore would surely die without ever having stained the blank pages with a single letter—what could have been the greatest book ever written.

So, too, is it with how we ourselves might choose to live. We can sit at home in our armchairs and wonder for quite some time about *why* we should live; in fact, we could wonder ourselves to death and still not know *why* with absolute certainty.

Here, we are faced with a dilemma: if we do not know *why*, then we also do not know *how*, as the *why* instructs the *how*. So, we are left paralyzed. Yet we must do something, mustn't we? But how do we know what to do if we do not know for what reason we do it? Mustn't everything have a reason?

If we cannot act without knowing *why*, but we cannot know *why*, at least not for certain, then, because there may be eternal consequences from our finite lives, we must decide *how* to act under uncertainty, lest we live paralyzed, not ever knowing for certain.

It would not necessarily be a bad existence, to sit in an armchair and do nothing but think for a lifetime, except that there are things we might otherwise do. We cannot afford the luxury of spending our lifetimes in armchairs theorizing about *why* because our finite lives may have eternal consequences.

Therefore, the key to finding purpose and living a meaningful life is not to uncover some hidden truth or answer and be certain and then live by it. We are not capable of this.

Instead, we must consider all uncertainties to make an uncertain decision and take uncertain action while we live, which positions us optimally to meet the certain truth, if such a thing exists, upon certain death—really the only certain thing.

Self-actualization, discovered by decision theory, solves the dilemma. Self-actualization, in this way, as a crutch, is less a purpose in and of itself than it is a means to any number of conceivable ends, a framework with guidelines for how to behave as if there is a purpose, to be best situated to take advantage of any number of purposes, one of which may prove true.

We cannot know for sure that self-actualization is what we should do, but we will not live long enough to consider all other possibilities. There may be consequences to our lives here on earth, so we cannot just spend all our time thinking about these questions.

We should spend our lives in a way that positions us to be most advantaged when meeting whatever we might find upon death. Under uncertainty, we decide to self-actualize.

## What is self-actualization?

Self-actualization is the motivating need to realize our full potential. It is the process of an individual becoming all that he can. It is a particular process, able to be mastered.

It is never an attained value. Self-actualization is not an external thing that we will one day catch and hold and then possess in ourselves. It is not a static condition. It is a pursuit and a process.

Self-actualization is a constant chase after the eventual reality of our ideal selves, to constantly be all that we can, as we continually realize that we are capable of becoming something even greater, more than what we previously believed.

Living, we are one step behind our full actualization. Only in death do we attain it, if we have remained one step behind our greatest potential selves for a lifetime, and then, finally, when there is nothing else we can conceivably do, we step into death, as all that we could have been: a good death.

It is a higher, arguably the highest, human desire. Especially for a man who is not hungry, homeless, in danger, socially estranged, or lacking satisfaction of any other basic need, surely he is concerned with nothing more than actualizing his self.

We dream of being an author until we write a best-selling novel, then of being an entrepreneur until we start a million-dollar company, and then of being a traveler until we have seen every country, and then one day we die and cannot dream any longer, and hopefully on that day we are all that we could have been.

Actualization is already in us, potentially, intangibly. We spend a lifetime pulling it out, making it real, like sucking soda through a straw, until the sucking makes that noise of emptiness between the cubes of ice at the bottom of the cup, and the cup is thrown away, like a body is buried, emptied of its contents, having been all that it could, satisfied the world like a soda.

Because that is what soda is for, to satisfy; and soda is not sad to no longer exist, for its molecular structure to be rearranged by intestinal acids, like our bodies decompose in soil, so long as it has satisfied, fulfilled its purpose, been all that it could. Then, the soda is happy to no longer exist, as we are happy to die, self-actualized.

### Each individual has great potential.

We are born equal, as blobs of brain matter and muscle fibers, barely more than nothing with the potential to be almost anything. Man is capable of as much as he can imagine, able to affect matter in a deterministic time-sensitive system, to shake the cosmos with his thoughts born of desire and made real by focused ability.

He is limitless, to achieve almost anything within the bounds of his humanity and specific to his actualized self; but he cannot achieve everything because he is not a god.

If man is aware of the potential within himself, how can he remain distracted? How can he work toward any goal other than the actualization of his self? We are designed against normalcy, ordered contrary to just average, created for more than what has been done.

How can we deny ourselves our own potential? I think only if we are unaware of it. I am convinced that no man aware of his potential is content to be ordinary, satisfied with mediocrity.

*Potential is like a balloon.*

The potential of an individual man is like a balloon that he inflates with each heave of his lungs; its radius lengthens like a timeline of his life, each micrometer another second.

The balloon stops expanding only when he stops breathing, but it does not deflate, at least not entirely. The rubber walls of the balloon represent his potential, not his actual self.

When he passes and his living breath no longer sustains the rubber walls at their inflated position, after he ceases to breathe and removes his mouth from the opening, the balloon walls shrink down to fit around what he had actually become before passing, as the air escapes to become nothingness; potential not realized is nothing.

After we pass and can no longer breathe actuality into our potential, our spaces in existence, our balloons, are reduced by the weight of the universe to the actuality with which they were filled.

If a man is completely self-actualized, his balloon does not shrink at all because its rubber walls are held in position, wrapped tightly around his fully actualized self—finite, static, after he has died, but existing forever, to hold up that space, that part of existence, to fill that pocket for eternity.

## Why we fail to realize our full potential.

Man has more potential than even he himself knows, able to be even more than his imagination. Yet most of us will never fully develop our potential, to become the person we dream of being, much less the person we did not even dare to dream of being, though we were nonetheless capable all along.

We are not aware or confident of the immense power within ourselves, so we hedge our bets and settle for average. So many fail to achieve, not because they are incapable, but because they do not know themselves—ignorant of their own needs and therefore lacking the motivation to focus their almost limitless human ability.

We fail to realize our wildest dreams, to become all that we can, not because we are inadequate or unable, not even necessarily in all cases because we are unwilling to make sacrifices or work hard, but rather because we are unaware of the process of actualization; in most cases, we lack the self-knowledge required to even begin the process, to generate powerful thoughts and harness the motivation of our needs in order to exercise our focused abilities.

We fail to realize our potential and actualize our thoughts most often simply because we do not know *how*.

### There is a very particular process to realizing potential.

The process of realizing potential is the process of self-actualization: how we bring intangible thought to physical reality so that we might become all that we can before dying.

We become anything or bring anything to reality, whether it be fame or fortune or any other sort of achievement, ultimately to actualize our potential, to make real our greatest future selves, by a particular process: first knowing ourselves, then harnessing the motivation of our needs and exercising our focused abilities.

### Rightness and goodness.

There are some deeper philosophical questions about self-actualization that we will not necessarily take up in this book, as they do not so much concern *how* or *why* we self-actualize, but more so what it means to self-actualize.

For example, does self-actualization require goodness? Or, does self-actualization require rightness? The answers to these questions are of little use in practicality.

A self-actualized religious person is as holy as he can be, having prayed as much as he is capable, but does self-actualization require that he has chosen a true religion? Is it possible that we become self-actualized based on a lie, or does it require truth?

A hedonist, by the process of self-actualization, most certainly maximizes his pleasure and minimizes his pain, but is being a hedonist a good thing? Is there something better that he might be, something more objectively good, and is the hedonist not self-actualized unless he realizes whatever is more objectively good?

A man wants to be rich, and does become rich, but what if he could have been an astronaut? And we deem being an astronaut to be greater than being rich. Is the rich man less than self-actualized for doing exactly what he wanted to do but less than he otherwise could have? Even if a man wants to become something, it does not necessarily mean that was all that he could have been.

Most people have their own beliefs, their own subjective *why*, their own frameworks. We are the same, but we are also very different, particularly when it comes to what we believe.

Therefore, self-actualization, as it is described in this book, is not so much a competing framework itself, as it is a means to the ends of any other framework

For the religious and scientists, hedonists and capitalists, whether you want to be happy, rich, powerful, or loved, the process of self-actualization taught by this book will show you how to become all that you want to be, but we will avoid questions about whether all that you want to be is right and good.

# PART ONE: HOW

# SELF-KNOWLEDGE

*BEGINNING OF ACTUALIZATION*

In part one, we will focus on *how* to self-actualize: beginning with Self-Knowledge, then Thought, which we bring to reality by use of Need and Ability, married to give birth to Focus.

❖❖❖

To become all that we can, to self-actualize, we must first learn about our human selves to determine the size of our potential spaces in existence and how we might go about filling those spaces.

Like an archer cannot hit a target that he cannot see, or if he does not have a bow and arrow and mastery of archery; man cannot satisfy the needs he does not know, or if he has not taken inventory of his natural abilities and learned to use them.

As Aristotle said, we become what we repeatedly do; therefore, self-knowledge for the purpose of actualization should be learned through the lens of what we might do and how we might do it, as we become anything by doing something, become more by doing more and all that we can by doing everything of which our human nature and finite lifetimes make us capable before we die.

The reason that we do not self-actualize, or fail in any other regard, is not that we are incapable; it is that we do not know ourselves. The process of actualization—knowing our needs and then focusing our known abilities for their satisfaction—can result only from first knowing these things about ourselves.

Self-actualization starts in the mind. A man aware of his own needs, especially his highest needs to which all lesser ones are subordinate, is motivated to focus his whole able person toward their satisfaction, and most always satisfies them, or dies trying.

*To know ourselves, we must grow up to live on our own.*

We cannot know ourselves without first thinking and living for ourselves, yet we are born into worlds that are not our own, where we believe in our parents' religion, learn our teachers' opinions, and act like our peers; where we eat food spooned onto our plates, wear clothes put on our backs, and sleep in beds made for us. We follow the rules for fear of disapproval and inevitably become who our elders want us to be.

In a world constructed by others that is not your own, the thoughts and needs and abilities that create your reality are theirs not yours. Without the full weight of your own existence yoked down onto your own shoulders, you cannot know yourself, and therefore cannot actualize what you do not know.

Self-knowledge, and therefore self-actualization, is impossible for us as children, born determined, incapable and unaware of ourselves, clumsy and needing tending to. Without the care of our elders we would die very young; our control is made inevitable by our helplessness as infants.

As a child, I learned to need what was expected of me. My desire for self-actualization was suppressed, overpowered by my social desires for familial love and communal acceptance. My foremost need was to be coddled. I did what my peers were doing, what would please my parents, what my mentors expected of me, and what would make others think best of me—but these things I did only to belong and feel loved.

I understood my needs, learned new abilities, evaluated my self worth, and built my identity according to the grades that teachers assigned to my intelligence, the rumors my peers whispered about my social status, and the pride my parents showed in response to my accomplishments.

This is childhood; it is necessary, our nature to be cared for in the early years, a beautiful and bliss-filled part of the human life, which certainly should not be stopped short or interrupted to begin earlier the process of self-actualization.

However, if our actions are subconsciously caused by the precepts taught to us as children that remain latent and unchallenged in our minds, then we are not living for ourselves.

After childhood, when our own abilities become capable of satisfying our own needs, when our desire to do something ourselves grows stronger than our desires for community and acceptance, we must then depart from the helplessness of infancy as soon as possible. We must escape to our own worlds where we can know ourselves and begin the process of actualization.

Some never grow up. Some leave their households only then to be taken care of by other communities. For example, a privileged child is born into a wealthy family, goes to boarding school, attends college and then graduates to work for a company. Such a person, always, in one way or another, cared for by a community, never feels the full weight of their own existence.

A childish man under the covers in the morning stays there to rest beneath the comfort of his safe sheets in the warmth of a soft dawning light. He is afraid to wake, to leave his dreams of another reality not so similar to hell as his own, because he has not grown, and remains incapable of beginning the process of actualization to make his dreams into reality.

But a grown man rises immediately because he must begin the work that is of utmost importance to himself and others; he rises earnestly to do it, because he is grown, no longer a child, living for himself, for a greater purpose.

### Limitless like gods. Limited as humans.

A man that studies for his whole life, a fruit fly, still does not know everything there is to know about that fruit fly, or a man that trains his whole life, to be strong, can still not move mountains.

Because we are not gods, not all knowing or all powerful, but still made in His likeness, like Einstein shared in His omniscience and Schwarzenegger shares in his omnipotence.

Our Creator allows us to live lifetimes as small segments of His infiniteness, endowed with a share of His omniscience in our minds capable of thought and a share of His omnipotence in our bodies capable of transferring our thoughts to reality.

Yet we are still limited, as mortals compared to God, as well as unequally advantaged members of mankind compared to one another. But even with limits, we must still self-actualize; in fact, without limits, self-actualization would not be possible, as our potential would be limitless and we could never realize it fully.

We are who we are; rather than waste time trying to change our natures to no avail—because again, we are not gods—we should become all that we can, first knowing our human selves as we are, even if we are lesser than we wish to be.

Self-knowledge empowers us, not to change the nature of ourselves, but to understand ourselves as we are, to learn how to take advantage of our humanity—bodies as machines operated by our minds—to travel far and press hard up against our limits, in order to become our best versions. Knowing our limits just well enough to modify our behavior so that we do not crash into them.

Like a cross country runner paces himself; he does not sprint from start to finish because if he runs too fast in the beginning his lungs and muscles will not sustain him to the end. But if he strategizes—runs quickly for a short while and then slows down to regain breath in his lungs and strength in his muscles before starting to run quickly again—then he is able to perform at peak efficiency, aware of himself, especially his limits.

Knowing our limits is part of knowing ourselves, yet we must not be so aware of our limits to become discouraged, but just barely aware, almost subconsciously. Just as the runner strikes a balance—arrogant to believe that he is capable of more, pressing harder, but also humble enough to know at some point he cannot go any further.

### Arrogance and humility: balance for self.

Knowing ourselves as godlike and limitless but still limited as humans we must balance between arrogance and humility.

We must be arrogant enough to believe that we are capable of actualizing our great potentials. This arrogance must be continual, as we grow stronger and more capable, so that we are able to constantly achieve what was impossible for our lesser selves.

We must be arrogant to spend time looking inward to develop ourselves as finely tuned machines. We must not doubt our great selves, but we must also be humble.

Arrogance is toxic if we begin to think ourselves greater than we actually are; on the other hand, too much humility harbors disbelief in that of which we would have otherwise been capable. The balance between arrogance and humility is fragile.

It allows us to develop a more realistic conception of ourselves, of potential that we are certainly able to actualize. With this balance, we are able to avoid unhappiness from desiring to be someone that we cannot ever be.

If we are less, then we must be humble to accept this. We must be humble to accept the reality that we are not gods and our spaces in existence are small, but only relatively, and no matter, because no man should worry about that which he is not.

For example, a man who works with his hands for minimal wages need not worry that he is not rich. He should work until his hands bleed and rejoice that he has pushed his body to its limits.

Even though he sees other men fulfilling purposes that seem to be greater than his own, he must be humble to actualize his potential for manual labor; but he must also simultaneously be arrogant enough to know if and when he is capable of more.

If he comes to believe that he is capable of more—of being rich, for example—and he deems a man with lots of money to be greater than a man who works with his hands, then he should cast down his tools at once and pursue riches.

This becomes a constant internal debate: whether his belief in himself to be capable of more is a realistic conception of his self, which he is actually capable of actualizing—and becomes his need, his duty even, to do so—or, whether it is a result of extreme hubris.

If it is pride, not potential, then he might expect to be met with failure, again and again, as he is simply not capable—something he would have presumably known beforehand if he had come to know himself well enough—then again, no matter how well we come to know ourselves, it is always possible that we are mistaken about what we are and are not capable of.

Even worse than the laborer trying and failing to do something more would have been for the laborer to conceive himself as less than what he actually could have been if he had only tried.

Imagine if Einstein had been too humble to think or if Shakespeare had been too humble to write. Must all amateurs then conceptualize themselves to be great, like a young scientist who aspires to theorize like Einstein or a young author that aspires to write like Shakespeare? What if we dared to dream for more even at almost certain risk of failure? It would make us unhappy, but we might achieve something for the greater good. Must we then dare to be more, to be arrogant, even at the cost of our happiness?

### Happiness and sacrifice.

If we are too arrogant, believing ourselves to have more potential than we actually do, then it is very difficult to actualize, and therefore very difficult to be happy. But this also makes possible achievements that would not have happened if we were more humble. If arrogance might allow us to achieve something our humble selves would otherwise have not, should we then err on the side of arrogance for the sake of achievement? Or, should we err on the side of humility for the sake of our own personal happiness?

If we are too humble, believing ourselves to have less potential than we actually do, then it is very easy to actualize, and therefore very easy to be happy. But this also makes impossible achievements that would have happened if we were more arrogant.

We are unhappy as less than we want to be, pressed up against a glass ceiling, able to see our desired heights, but unable to ascend there: a poor man that wants be rich, a nameless man that wants to be famous, a foolish man that wants to be wise, a weak man that wants to be strong.

If happiness is highly correlated with self-actualization, should we then aspire to be less in order to be happy? Should we conceptualize ourselves conservatively to increase our chances of self-actualization, guaranteeing ourselves more happiness at the cost of what we might have otherwise achieved?

Or, might we sacrifice balance and happiness to be arrogant for the possibility of achieving more than our humble selves, chasing after what we might never achieve? Like shooting for the moon at high risk of a lifetime of constant dissatisfaction spent alone in cold, dark space. Is that risk worth a chance at doing something more?

If we constantly want more, continually motivated to keep working, then we will rarely be happy as we are unable to satisfy our desire for self-actualization. Might our achievements be worth our happiness? Well, maybe; if we are able to help others, able to increase their happiness, even if it means sacrificing our own.

If what we as humans—both as individuals and as our whole race together—might be able to achieve is important enough, then we must be arrogant enough to at least try, even if the most likely outcome is failure. We must choose: whether to be happy or to sacrifice for others, striving for what our arrogant selves might achieve that our humble selves certainly would not.

# THOUGHT

## GOD-LIKE CREATIVE POWER OF MAN

Thoughts are powerful things, existing somewhere between real and unreal, intangible but with great potential for being made into physical reality. Thought will be the beginning of everything that comes to exist, just as all that presently exists was once thought.

Just as reality was born from the divine thought of the original Creator, thought is the force that now still continually shapes and sustains reality, as humanity, divinely endowed with god-like creative faculties, interacts with the original creation of the unmoved Mover. Since the birth of mankind we have been steered and molded by the collective thoughts of individual men—some, all, or none of whom may have been divinely inspired.

As inconsequential as these metaphysical musings may seem to how we presently live—and therefore irrelevant to the central tenets of this book—they are, in fact, the foundational ideas necessary to achieving anything, creating a world that we are happy to live in, and creating ourselves as all that we can be.

### Thoughts as desires.

First, you must have a thought, an unreal thing capable of being made real. Then, gaining motivation, as a fire burns in your physical self like an engine revs in a machine, your body is caused to behave in certain ways, exercising focused use of your abilities to realize your thoughts. For humans, this process of our thoughts being actualized sometimes seems to occur automatically.

It is easiest to imagine for thoughts that are essentially desires. For example, consider our impulse to think of food as we become hungry and then most certainly find food, or starve and die; we rarely die of starvation because we desire so ravenously to live, and therefore think constantly about food and how else to survive.

With a thoughtful mind and an able body you can do most anything. If you want to be attractive, first hold it in your mind—this conception, this thought of your attractive self—then exercise and eat healthy, and surely it is soon made real.

If you want to be popular, first think, and then study the social mannerisms of popular peers. If you want to be smart—well, in this case, I suppose the requirement of thought is rather obvious. If you want to be rich, work. If you want to write a book, then write.

One truly brilliant thought is the difference between your greater and lesser self, between a greater and lesser world. For example, the wheel, printing press, and computer—all now very much physical things that began as thoughts.

We often take the physical process to be the more difficult of the two parts, but we are often mistaken. If we are to hold a desire as a thought in our minds and become motivated, the physical process then becomes very nearly automatic. In some ways, thought, especially in the form of desire, is very real despite its intangibility, as its immaterial potential is typically almost certain to become reality.

After having had a thought, if it is the desire of the thinker that the thought be made real, then the human process begins, by which thoughts are actualized. Our human bodies, instructed by our desirous thoughts, are designed to take care of the process.

We must only remember that it all begins with thought. If we desire to be powerful, we must learn to harbor powerful thoughts.

### Thought shapes our reality by creation and perception.

Whatever man is able to conceive in his mind he is certainly able to make real. Our thoughts create the world around us and we can create any world that we desire.

Our thoughts construct our reality in two ways: by creation and perception. Our minds are both the creative sculptors of our own reality and the lenses through which we see reality as however we choose to perceive it.

For example, I thought one day I'd write a book. That thought created the page filled with text that is now the subject of your perception as you read.

Anything in the physical world was first intangible thought, before being made real as the mind instructed a physical body to interact with matter in order to create something. That reality is then recreated by perception in the mind of any given beholder.

In this way, reality is continually created and recreated, perceived by thought, reshaped again and again, seen in different ways by different people with different perspectives.

Thought, as both creation and perception, governs what exists and does not exist, constructing each of our individual realities—products of what we ourselves create and make real, as well as how we perceive whatever we, and others, have created.

### Thought creates our selves.

In the same way that our thoughts create the world around us, so too do they create ourselves, as however we conceive ourselves, becoming whoever we constantly reimagine ourselves to be.

Yet we are so often unable to become our ideal selves, to manifest the great person we dream ourselves capable of becoming. For example, many of us think to make a great fortune, but so few succeed to become wealthy.

On the face of it, we are seemingly unable because we grow tired of working, afraid of failure, unwilling to spend enough time alone to accomplish what is necessary, to make sacrifices of pleasure for pain. But this is all a guise for a deeper cause.

Surely we are unable because we are distracted by our human needs and hindered by our mortal inabilities. If not for our humanity, everything we think would be, every thought immediately realized—*realized* in the most literal sense, to be made real.

If we were omnipotent, we would will into existence hundred dollar bills, spontaneously generating and bending matter in order to instantly create paper currency from thin air—this is how I imagine the power of the original Creator.

Even without omnipotence, we as men are still powerful; above all else, we are unable simply because we do not know ourselves and have not yet mastered the creative power of thought.

In a sense, we are capable of bending matter; only the process is much slower. We must work within the framework of our humanity, unable to necessarily bend matter, but certainly able to learn and develop our marketable skills in order to work for wages as employees or for profits as entrepreneurs in a functioning economy.

There is no sense in rebelling against our humanity and social institutions; it is foolish to fight against who we are, because it is our nature, which we cannot change. But we can learn our intricacies and how to operate them.

We can work with our seeming human disadvantages to turn them into advantages, like our finiteness inclines us to self-actualize and our constant human need motivates us. This is why we must know ourselves, becoming intimately aware of our minds in relation to our bodies, to wield power that is inherent to the human self.

## Cogito ergo sum: we are our minds.

As Descartes said, I think therefore I am. We are more than our bodies, more than our physical shells. You are not you because of your feet, like I am not I because of my hands and a stranger is not whoever they are because of their face.

For example, if there was a man named John, and John lost both his legs in an accident, we would not necessarily say that John is any less himself. John is everything that he previously was, minus his legs. What remains of his physical self we still call John, because his arms, torso, and head are all still controlled by his mind.

If, however, John had died in the accident, and his body was intact, but it was a lifeless corpse, then we would likely say that John has passed from this life, that John is no longer here.

We are not our bodies; we are the life within our bodies, which seems to be inextricably linked to our minds—the part of us responsible for generating thought.

You are you because of your mind, the intangible part of yourself that Homer called *psyche*. How exactly your brain processes information is what makes you who you are, what causes whoever you were to become whoever you will be.

We are our minds; our bodies are the vehicles of our minds, how our minds experience reality. Our bodies are links between our minds and the physical world, modems between our intangible ideas and the real stuff of the real world.

Therefore, our thoughts are everything. Our bodies manifest, almost automatically, our thoughts, especially desires. We are designed to pursue what we need, to desire unmet needs, motivated to satisfy ourselves. We think what we do and do what we think.

This barely scratches the surface of a classic debate about the mind-body problem, which we cannot afford the time to digress and discuss in its entirety, but the point is that our minds and the thoughts they produce are very important to our human selves.

### Mind and thought are greater than body and strength.

How much lesser is the greatest athlete than the greatest thinker? What good are memories of muscle compared to memories of mind? The large arm of a great thrower of the discus, well learned in the sport, rots in the soil. Yet the genius of a great mind is transferrable, recordable, and able to stand the test of time.

Granted, the most powerful bodies must certainly be results of powerful minds. A great athlete does not become that way without a strong mind. Physical excellence certainly requires knowledge of self to diligently practice, as well as knowledge of the sport.

Many athletes use their physical excellence, as a result of their powerful minds, to realize their desires, achieving immortality through their legacies that live on due to their greatness in sport.

Still, a body built up for physical feats dies in the ground just the same as weaker bodies, while a mind swelling with brilliance is made immortal by its inventions, writings, and recorded thoughts.

Abilities of the body produce less utility than abilities of the mind. A body, no matter how strong, dies in the ground. A mind lives on through its eternal thought.

*Remember and forget: balance of thought.*

What happens to a thought forgotten, like a road not traveled or a dream deferred? Nothing. A thought forgotten never was, if it was never transmuted to reality by any sort of action. Not written, or even spoken, a thought forgotten only ever had the capacity and potential to exist, but never actually existed.

Like a road not traveled. If you only ever stood at the foot of it, and you were then blindfolded and spun in circles and afterwards the road was gone and you cannot remember what it looked like.

Like a dream deferred. If you had a dream but woke and could not remember, then it was nothing more than a figment of your imagination fated to die in your subconscious.

What if one thought forgotten was the greatest thought you would ever have, but you just ignored it, because you were busy, preoccupied, or distracted? What's more important than your greatest thought? What makes a thought justifiably forgotten? What amount of greatness is negligible?

There are other roads, but with only so many steps to walk you must find balance between walking a great number of roads and walking a great distance down any given road.

There are other thoughts, but you can only remember so much, only think so many thoughts. Sometimes it's best to spend brainpower trying to remember, other times it's better to turn to the next inevitable thought. You have incentive to forget; in pursuit of greatness, however, you must also remember.

We must balance what we forget with what we remember, forgetting some thoughts to remember better thoughts, thinking about some things instead of other things, remembering any thought just long enough to know whether it is a great thought, greater than all those about which we might otherwise think.

*Deep and shallow: more balance.*

Just as we balance the thoughts we remember with those we forget, we must also balance deep thoughts with shallow thoughts.

We must think on a level not so deep as to run down rabbit holes but not so shallow as to run the risk of being common and irrelevant.

This balance allows us to arrive at a deeper understanding that is still shallow enough to be commonly accessible, complex enough to be important but simple enough to be useful.

Like swimming in the ocean in the shallow waters amongst the fishermen that are like us in their boats, only occasionally diving deeper beneath the surface from where the sun shines through to the pressure and darkness below, to deeper waters where we learn from monstrous thoughts in their caves, before resurfacing to catch our breath and tell the fishermen what we learned.

Like looking through the forest to see its trees, but also knowing the trees together to be a forest, with its trees like many separate thoughts, together a greater picture. No individual tree is grown up too high into the clouds or roots grown too deep into the soil. Rather, many trees, their branches of common heights and roots at normal depths. Together, these trees, balanced with one another, are all generally accessible to the common traveler.

Because one man could spend a lifetime studying a fruit fly, and just before his death still not know everything that there is to know about that fruit fly, and even then: of what use to him was all that knowledge of a fruit fly?

### Esoteric: the tragedy of genius.

I cannot know for sure, as I myself have not reached such a level of intellect and likely never will, but I imagine there must come a point when a very intelligent man becomes too smart for his own good, or for any good—when his knowledge is too esoteric, useless to the layman. When he forgets what it was like to see the world through the lens of his more common, less brilliant mind.

It is particularly important then, for one who seeks to think thoughts that might be socially useful, to be careful about running down rabbit holes, chasing after ideas that no longer resonate with the public. His deeper understanding must still be shallow enough to be commonly accessible; it must be complex enough to be important but simple enough to be useful.

For what purpose is there in writing or philosophy or any knowledge, or this book even, if it does not enable us to live better lives? Of course there are certain complex topics—scientific theories, mathematic calculations—that yield great benefits for society, which need not be understood by everyone so long as the knowledge is sufficiently explained to the next generation of thinkers in the field.

However, knowledge of how to live—the type which this book hopes to possess—must be confined to what resonates with the common man and written in such a way that is concise and easily understood, if it is to have any sort of impact or usefulness.

Otherwise, esoteric knowledge passed down by the pedant scholars of each generation and taught only to students of higher education fails to be useful or produce any good for the majority of each generation of mankind.

Therefore, in discussions and writings about how we might live there must be a balance between subject matter that will be heard or read because it is applicable and understandable, and content with enough precision and complexity to be original and useful.

In this way, a great part of brilliance, in addition to understanding higher truths, resides in an ability to communicate such truths in a commonly accessible language. I suppose this must be why Einstein held simplicity in such high regard.

### Steal like a genius: gain powerful thoughts from others.

If your own mind is not a powerful generator of thought, then steal from others. Conversation, preferably with those smarter than yourself, is the key to gaining knowledge from other minds when your own fails to produce great ideas.

Your brain is like a pool of investments where assets are knowledge instead of money. The pool begins as the total amount of your own personal funds, most of which is probably from your parents. You are the first investor.

First, learn about your personal funds and the assets in which they are invested, your thoughts and their schools. Next, attract other investors by promising them returns of your own knowledge. Approach those interested in your thoughts, which they do not yet possess. The transaction is made by conversation or writing, offering more of your own knowledge until you have received most of theirs, moving money from their pockets to yours.

Now smarter, with a pool of investments marginally larger and diversified, you can approach investors with more knowledge in more schools of thought. This becomes a process: approaching increasingly smarter investors, having been made smarter yourself again and again by the previous round of investors.

It is stealing only in the sense that you gain immensely at the cost of nothing more than your time to make the transaction, to have a conversation. Otherwise it is mutually beneficial: both parties gain knowledge that they did not previously possess.

This strategy works because knowledge is a quasi-public good, a resource that benefits more people without decreasing its value. For example, many different people can read copies of the same book at the same time and attain the same knowledge, but only one person can possess one dollar at one point in time; in other words, two thinkers can simultaneously take action based on the same bit of knowledge, whereas the spending power of a dollar with a unique serial number cannot be used by two actors simultaneously.

While in-person conversation only grants access to the knowledge of those presently alive, many of the most brilliant minds before us have been immortalized in writing, their books arguably even cheaper than the time otherwise spent gaining knowledge by conversation with living persons.

The kind of genius that results from this strategy is not necessarily specialized like a man who knows a great deal about one particular topic or trade, nor is it natural like savants or prodigies; it is one man learning to think like many men all at once.

Like a whole economy in one mind with thousands of units of intellectual capital seamlessly and efficiently producing brilliance by the synergistic powers of multi-disciplinary thought. Or, like a summit of philosophers gathered to debate, but the debate is internal without lapses in conversation or delays for ideas to be formed into word and spoken, because all minds are present in one mind.

With enough time, a man that executes this strategy quickly and efficiently becomes one of the smartest men in the world.

*Wolves and sheep: self-education and formal schooling.*

This section is different from others in the chapter as it is not so relevant to thought on a higher level; instead, it focuses through a practical, modern lens on how we, especially our youth, now think.

See, in school I became very good at absorbing information and holding my breath until it oozed out of my ears, regurgitated onto my exam papers and filled into bubbles, which is very different, I thought, from how things are achieved in the real world.

Formal education seems inefficient to me. We forget so much of what we learn. Why do we spend so long storing up information in our heads and wait so many years to use it for production? Why not, instead, learn then execute and then learn whatever else we need to continue executing and reiterating?

Many powerful thoughts are generated by those resistant to syllabi, attendance policies, and other semantics, those bored by memorization and recitation of longstanding theories.

So many brilliant and creative minds have developed outside of formal schooling that it seems there is a limit to its effectiveness, especially once basic principles have been learned. This limit must be what inclines the greatest students to work independently of their education systems to ascend beyond them.

Original ideas are suffocated in a mind learned from lecture of constructs so clearly defined. Formal education is destructive of creativity; am I wrong to think this is the opposite of what it should be, that our universities should be havens for originality?

School prepares us as employees to sit in a chair at a desk for long hours, to take instructions and meet deadlines. School teaches us to be less than what we could otherwise be. Formal education instructs us to be only that which is required in the job description for whomever we might work, but we can be so much more.

I used to want to be a banker, to make lots of money. I would have spent my adult life collecting green papers as if they were anything but fuel for my incessantly burning ego.

But there have been many rich bankers before me; one of my peers will surely take my place and a student of the next formally educated generation will surely take his.

# NEED AND ABILITY
*PROCESS OF ACTUALIZATION*

I have an immense and unshakeable belief in the power of an individual man: first, to have a thought, and then, by just a short bout of focused ability, motivated by need, to make real, bring to reality, that thought, which had existed previously only in his mind.

To self-actualize, chasing after our ideal future selves, we must understand two parts of our present selves: need and ability.

Needs are similar to wants or desires, sources of motivation, inclinations to pursue what we require. Abilities are similar to skills or powers, how we satisfy our needs, realize what we want, and acquire what we desire. Needs and abilities, together, are the two main determinants of whether we will self-actualize.

Our intangible minds instruct our physical bodies how to interact with time and space. A particular process of achievement optimizes this interaction, the instruction of the mind to the body and the response of the body to the mind. This interaction, between the mind and the body, is governed primarily by need and ability.

It is a system like a machine. Our need is the source of motivation, like cause; our ability is how we satisfy need, like means; and the effect then, of need combined with ability, is what we do— the ends of our motivations fueled by unmet needs realized as a result of the focused use of our abilities.

## Man like machine.

Our bodies are machines operated by our minds. Machines, like men, have needs and abilities, input requirements that make them capable of operating to produce output.

An automobile, for example, is a machine whose nature is to be driven. But with a child in the driver's seat an automobile is nothing more than the metal of its frame and the rubber of its tires, as the child is likely not able even to turn the key in the ignition.

A very intelligent man with knowledge of everything, except for automobiles, is just as useless to the machine as the child. Despite the machine's great potential for speed and the man's great brilliance of all other things, they sit idle. It may even be dangerous for such power to be in the hands of one with no knowledge of how to use it.

An automobile's operator must know the machine both as a mechanic and driver. If its operator is not intelligent as a mechanic, unable to fix a broken engine or change the tires, the automobile will degenerate and become less than capable of all that it previously was.

If its operator is not intelligent as a driver, unable to step on the gas pedal or shift gears, even if maintained to operate efficiently, the automobile is unable to actualize its potential power.

Great machines built to operate with immense power are only as good as their operators and their operators are only as good for the machine as their specialized knowledge of its operations. A beautiful, powerful, capable machine becomes useless in the hands of someone without knowledge of its intricacies.

Just as we, our minds, must know our bodies like machines, to operate at peak efficiency, to be powerful, to produce greatness. Without intimate knowledge of our machines we cannot operate them; or, even worse, we might operate them poorly, dangerously.

Therefore, we must know ourselves, our needs and abilities, as intimately as possible, like a driver must know his automobile, to race at top speed toward the finish line.

### Need and ability as hunger and hunting.

Like an automobile without a driver goes nowhere, need and ability, separate from one another, cause nothing.

Consider, for example, hunger as need and hunting as ability. Men behave differently according to their needs and abilities— whether they are hungry or satisfied and able or not able to hunt.

(1) A hungry man able to hunt surely kills and eats to satisfy his hunger, but without both need and ability to acquire food, nothing is necessarily done. (2) A hunter able to hunt but already satisfied with a full belly will not hunt because he has no need.

(3) A man who is unable to hunt but already satisfied with a full belly will also not hunt. (4) But a hungry man, in need of food and stranded alone in the wilderness, who is unable to hunt, assuming that hunting is his only means to acquire food, will not satisfy his need for food and will starve and die.

However, a fifth scenario can be imagined where, if given enough time before he dies of starvation, the hungry man unable to hunt learns to hunt very quickly, focusing all of his self to develop the one ability necessary to satisfy his foremost need for survival. He learns to hunt and eats his kill to survive.

This learned ability is a result of focus, a result of acute awareness of need combined with knowledge of potential ability and the availability of resources to actualize that potential.

This is the key to unlocking our full potential. This is how we artificially push our limits and achieve beyond our natural abilities, expanding our actual present natures further outward toward the bounds of our future potential selves, by becoming aware of our needs, especially those necessary for our survival, and then learning the abilities to satisfy our needs—just like the hungry man.

### Need is motivation.

Like a hungry man in the wilderness becomes a hunter, what we become, what we learn, that of which we become capable, all results from what we need. If we had not been created as social animals needing human interaction, then we might not have learned to speak; similarly, if we did not need to self-actualize, then we might not have learned to work and achieve.

As Maslow said, a hungry man lives by bread alone. Like a man held under water, in the moment that he cannot breathe, lives by air alone. Man becomes what he must in order to be capable of attaining that which he needs.

Self-actualization is more than just a question of ability but also a question of need because we are able to do best what we are most motivated to do and we are most motivated to do what we most need. Our own particular needs, specific to each of our selves, are the sources of our motivation. Knowing these needs that motivate us is the starting point of actualization. Everything begins with our needs.

In order to achieve we must be motivated, and in order to be motivated we must be ravenously and wretchedly unsatisfied, always needing more, in constant danger and awfully uncomfortable, hungry like animals, hunting for the kill that will sustain our lives.

### Self-actualization is the highest human need.

Psychologists and doctors of human behavior argue about what exactly are our needs and how they are ordered, especially relative to one another. We clearly need to eat and to drink in order to sustain our life processes but less clear are our needs like love and esteem, those related to the more intangible parts of our selves.

Most human needs are innate, but we also develop needs for things of which we were not previously aware. These ideas come to us from our environments. Like eating chocolate for the first time and thereafter developing a need for chocolate.

Our most powerful needs are of a higher order. It seems these higher needs are related to *why*, while our lesser needs are related to *how*, and our still lesser needs are related to *what*.

Higher needs are often disguised as lower needs, like sex is more than just physical but also for love, or money is more than its spending power but also for esteem.

Lower needs must only be stepping-stones or catalysts or a reward system for our higher order needs. We must elevate our needs to a higher order for more powerful motivation.

It seems our highest need is self-actualization. From our nature, it seems that we were created to do something more than just live and die, but to exist with very particular conditions that might incline us to make something of our existence, to achieve something.

Otherwise we might live infinitely without needs or abilities. Just as it seems we must do something because we are finite, because we will die and lose the opportunity to do anything thereafter, it seems we must do something also because we are born unsatisfied, with needs that require constant satisfaction, lest we die anyhow.

These desires, ultimately as the desire to stay alive, motivate us to do something rather than nothing. We are born to achieve; it is our nature. We are ordered to it, made desirous of it and even capable of attaining it, so that we might actualize ourselves.

### *Abilities are secondary to our needs.*

We are constantly unsatisfied creatures; therefore we must do things to satisfy ourselves. Our needs motivate us to do these things, but the doing itself is less important than what causes the doing.

Needs are the beginning, then our abilities follow almost automatically. Our needs cause our abilities. We become able to satisfy unmet needs by learning new abilities if old abilities are not sufficient. Therefore, needs are more important than abilities.

### Our abilities are limited.

We are limited as humans. Even just before death, as motivated as possible to do whatever he might to survive, a man is still unable to do some things. Even if maximally motivated, needing ravenously to survive even, our abilities are still limited.

Even if otherwise dying, a man is still unable to lift up mountains, swim across the ocean, or jump to the moon. Nor is he able to know what exists at the bounds of the universe, what lives inside a black hole, or even all there is to know about a fruit fly.

Like a hungry man in need of food stranded alone in the wilderness may still not satisfy his need for food, if he is still unable to learn quickly enough to hunt well, or if he is just unlucky and unsuccessful, failing to make a kill, and he then starves and dies.

With time we can increase our abilities, motivated to learn and become better, like a hungry man learns to become a hunter. But even with lifetimes to learn, we are still limited—we must be humble to remember this but also arrogant to push our limits, expanding our potential until ultimately actualizing our true, ideal selves.

# FOCUS

*MARRIAGE OF NEED AND ABILITY*

Our needs constantly demand satisfaction, motivating us to use and further develop our abilities—during this process, man is said to be focused. Like a hungry man unable to hunt focuses and learns to hunt very quickly, developing the one ability necessary to satisfy his foremost need for survival.

Focus is essential to self-actualization; it allows us to achieve beyond what our natural abilities make possible, expanding our present natures toward the limits of our potential future selves.

For the common man, abilities continually developed by focus are those most requisite for his greatest achievements, unlike savants and prodigies—those born naturally with abilities greater than what most men can achieve even after a lifetime of focus.

With great natural ability but little need and therefore no focus, a man is unlikely to realize his full potential, only ever becoming just marginally more actualized than the day he was born.

But with immense focus as a result of little natural ability combined with great need, a man can become anything, like a runner that starts far behind but then accelerates quickly to pass the others.

## We are naturally unfocused.

We are born distracted and lacking focus, pulled in many directions by a multitude of needs. A typical man is satisfied in many different ways: eating to satisfy hunger, exercising to keep his body in shape and maintain self-esteem, talking to his peers to satisfy social desires, committing his time to his work to self-actualize.

At any point, the whole of a man's motivation is pulled in many different directions towards different pursuits, each of which he imagines will satisfy a different one of his needs.

But a man is capable of only so much when pulled in so many different directions as a lesser amount of his ability is given to each additional pursuit; therefore, in order to achieve greatness, more than just mediocrity, he must wrap up all of his needs into few pursuits, maximally focusing his use of ability for the satisfaction of those needs, motivating him to achieve those few pursuits.

### Writing as an example of focus.

Writing this book, I have learned the value of committing my whole self to a project—one so important it is worth stopping all other pursuits to chase after obsessively. It has created a void in my life that I might fill afterwards with something else of importance, lest I begin to feel very bored each day and wonder about what to do.

Many hours I have spent alone, chiseling away excess, sculpting, until each sentence, paragraph, and eventually the entire book takes the greatest form I am capable of creating.

Writing, I learned of complete obsession with one pursuit and entire disinterest in everything else, denying myself many things that previously occupied much of my time. I am now able to sit hungry and tired for longer, less bothered by physiological needs.

Sometimes I sit down to write and consider for a moment that I could start and not stop, so motivated in that moment I feel as if I could work for days, weeks even, without stopping.

Then, for an hour, sometimes two or three, I work hard and fast with intense focus, music blocking out noise, caffeine steadying my hands, eyes glued to the pages, until my stomach grumbles, my muscles need stretching, and I lose focus, distracted by my needs: comfort, hunger, thirst, loneliness, fatigue.

### Humanity both as essential to and destructive of focus.

Our needy humanity is the greatest barrier to the focus of our supernatural minds instructing our physical bodies; yet these human elements are also simultaneously the parts of our selves that make focus possible in the first place.

We are inconvenienced by our mortality, distracted from focusing on work that seems to be the purpose of our existence by human needs that we can satisfy only by spending the time we might otherwise spend actualizing ourselves and producing for others.

This is annoying, that we must spend time surviving, satisfying our human needs, consuming instead of producing; yet there is little use grumbling about this tragedy. It is certainly our nature that we cannot escape, so we must discover how to most efficiently make use of our time, reducing our consumption to the minimum of what is necessary to continue producing.

There is no shortcut for focus. It takes patience and time, but focus is irreplaceable in the process of actualization. If you can work for most hours of each day, every day, focused on one task, nothing will keep you from success. So how can we artificially create focus?

## *A focused mind is free from lower needs of the body.*

In order to focus you must keep from consciousness as much of your humanity as possible. The key is to allow the mind to operate free from the naggings of body discomfort. Physical needs must be reduced to only that which optimizes performance.

Each body is different; each of us has our own environment that allows for a supreme level of focus. My own environment is very particular but can be recreated in most locations:

The light must be bright but not too bright, symmetrical on either side of my line of sight and evenly distributed all around me. The temperature must be high but not too high, enough at least to relax my muscles and take my mind off of temperature entirely. Better that I be sweating than shivering; sweating at least allows my hands to remain steady. Coffee and music are also very helpful. Caffeine has its greatest effect early in the morning before breakfast. Music depends on the type of work. For qualitative, word-intensive work, the music must be non-lyrical and soft. For technical, number-intensive work, the music can be lyrical, loud and upbeat.

*A focused mind produces much and consumes little.*

Though we often think of consuming what we possess, what we possess often consumes us. When consumed by our possessions, we cannot produce and certainly cannot self-actualize.

All that we possess comes at a cost. Our belongings are purchased at a price and require our time for maintenance; money is made as wages in return for hours of work; relationships are sustained by our time spent with another and come with obligations. Memories, ideas, and dreams survive with brainpower, consuming our finite amount of thought each day.

Therefore, we must be careful about what we possess: belongings, money, relationships, obligations, and thoughts. Clutter is a deterrent to focus. In reality, we need very little to survive, consuming only what we need to continue producing—this includes how we consume the time of each day.

The most focused man, most capable of achievement, possesses very few physical things, social interactions, and thoughts. Possessing less, a man has more to spend, and is therefore able to produce much more, especially for others.

For example, a man with very few scheduled events and obligations is able to spend his time on his own, working on what is important to his self. Or, a man with few physical belongings has less to clean, fix, and organize, especially if he wishes to pick up and leave, he can do so with just the contents of several bags.

*A focused mind spends time alone.*

You must deny your social needs like you must deny your needs for physical belongings. You must worry only about the few variables that are necessary for your success and actualization. You must become comfortable with spending long hours alone.

Like a man made blind after having once seen, a focused mind works in darkness for periods of time, devoid of most human needs to produce what his distracted human self could not, so long as what he produces while in the dark is still created based on his memories of humanity in order to confer utility to others.

To have any meaningful long-term success you must do it yourself. You must become comfortable working long hours alone, relying only on your own mind and abilities.

You can bring an idea to an engineer but the engineer will be the proprietor of the product. You can connect two people but their partnership will thank and then forget you. You must be the engine to your own operations, treating partners just as accessories.

When striving to become the best person you can be, does your own company not become that which you most enjoy anyhow?

This solitude, however, must exist within a community, or at least with the possibility of future interaction. Stranded on an island with no hope of escape, I would hope to die quickly. I would not focus to work or create or invent because who would consume my production? What's anything good for if not for others?

## A focused mind ignores social anxiety.

We think too often about what everybody else thinks and not often enough about what we think ourselves. We are raised to be socially anxious, taught to spend time each day conducting ourselves so that others might perceive us a certain way.

Growing up, I cared too much about what people thought and was never able to focus on my work. I made decisions based on preconceived notions of what would be acceptable. I made choices based on how I thought they would make others think about me. My actions resulted from the thoughts of others, not my own.

Then I realized: everyone is too busy worrying about you thinking of them to even begin thinking about you. In reality, most people are too self-conscious to pay attention to anyone else.

Our worry about what others think is relative to proximity. We never worry about what a stranger on the other side of the world thinks about us, but we worry constantly about what our family, friends, classmates and coworkers think of us.

Why does it matter? What difference does it make what somebody thinks of you, particularly if that person is of little consequence to your life? Changing yourself for the approval of others is a slippery slope to irrelevance, destroying your unique individuality, as well as your progress toward self-actualization.

We cannot, however, be totally ignorant of the opinion of others, particularly the opinions of those qualified to comment intelligently on our work, but only so much before it becomes counterproductive. We should worry only about actualizing ourselves, not about what others worry about. Just because we see others worrying does not mean that we should be worrying too.

### *Maximum focus: one pursuit to satisfy all needs.*

A man aware of himself and consumed completely by one need, motivated to use all of his abilities and ignore all other needs in order to achieve one particular goal—does he not achieve it?

If the desire obsesses him, even to neglect food and drink, to forego social interaction and deny himself all other pleasantries until he achieves this particular goal, then he must certainly achieve it.

If all of his abilities are directed toward one pursuit that will simultaneously satisfy all of his needs, then he becomes supremely motivated and therefore maximally focused on this one pursuit. This one pursuit must have the potential to satisfy all needs, besides those lower needs that he can afford to ignore temporarily.

A man achieves maximum motivation, all the focus of which he is capable, when committing himself to one subject of work that will solve all of his problems, simultaneously satisfying all of his needs: hunger, sex, safety, acceptance, respect, love, identity, fame, fortune, and actualization. All this, if he can only achieve one thing.

Like an animal backed into a corner with no option other than to fight for his life, a man that is maximally focused surely achieves the object of his focus, just as the animal will surely survive.

An ordinary man becomes extraordinary when consumed completely by one desperate need that he wants to satisfy more than anything else, and it demands the focus of his entire set of abilities.

For example, a hungry, tired student working at his desk late at night refuses to eat or sleep because his studies are essential to the love he needs from his parents and the esteem he needs from his peers, as well as the identity and self-actualization for his self.

Even more basic than love and esteem and actualization, the food he will eat at the dining halls the next morning and the bed he will eventually crawl into that night are provided by the university conditional upon his academic performance.

For several hours he works in the night while his classmates sleep, the whole of his present existence focused on the papers within the circle of light created by his desk lamp. His studies are the one pursuit essential to the actualization of his completely satisfied self.

We can artificially create focus: ordering all needs nagging at the mind behind one point of satisfaction, convincing the mind that everything its body requires is dependent on achieving the object of focus. It is then in the best interests of all parts of the human person to devote their faculties to the one pursuit.

## Death as an example of maximum focus.

A man beneath water needs air, so he rises above the surface or drowns and sinks to the bottom. If a man needs one thing more than anything else, even life itself, then he achieves it or dies trying.

To survive is our greatest need; death is the greatest motivator. It grants us maximum focus, aligning all abilities of the body to satisfy its need for survival, as well as every other need that might arise thereafter if it is to survive in that moment.

All that you could ever potentially need is pushed into that instant; all your abilities are pushed into your capacities in that moment just before what might have otherwise been death. But you survive, because you have to, like the hungry man who is unable to hunt learns to hunt and survives by eating his kill, his need for food satisfied by his learned ability to hunt.

In that moment of complete focus, things are simple. All that exists is the object of your focus. Your whole existence is wrapped up into one ultimate need in that very instant for that very thing.

# PART TWO: WHY

# DEATH

*THE "WHY" THAT DRIVES US*

Before, in part one, we focused on *how* to self-actualize, discussing Self-Knowledge, Thought, Need, Ability, and Focus. Now, in part two, we will turn our focus to *why* we should self-actualize.

❖❖❖

Thinking about death helps us appreciate life, like looking into darkness for a little while then looking back to light and being almost blinded by its suddenly intense brightness.

Like a wealthy man appreciates his riches more after having spent time with the poor, or like a healthy man appreciates his strength after having been sick. So too does a living man appreciate his life after having seriously considered death.

Thinking about death too often leads to fear and anxiety, but thinking about death too little breeds a treacherous and deceitful sense of immortality that coaxes us quickly to our ends.

Death might even teach us about how we should presently live. Like we learn about some things by thinking about what they are not, so too can we learn about life by thinking about its absence.

Death is the absence of life like dark is the absence of light. Death is all around us; time eats away at our lives like a flame burns along a wick. It is the one thing that affects us all just the same and binds us together regardless of nationality, religion, age, gender, political affiliation, or socioeconomic status. For as much as we are different, death makes us very similar, makes us human.

If you are reading this, surely you are alive, just as I am alive as I now write this—though as you now read, I may be dead, and that would be a beautiful thing, for this book to have lived on after me.

## Animal death.

Death is not unique to man. Animals, plants, and microbes suffer ends to their biological processes. As organisms, we inevitably die by termination of the biological functions that sustain our living selves, whether by old age, sickness, or some sort of accident.

We most often think of death this way—when we shut our eyes, our heart stops beating, lungs stop heaving and we go to sleep, buried in the ground or burned to ashes, unable to wake again.

We are animals, desiring to be fed and to drink and to be safe, but we are also humans, living to be all that we can, desiring to exist, in some sense, even past our finite lifetimes.

To be human is more than just surviving as a living organism: lungs breathing, heart beating, brain synapses firing to instruct the body how to satisfy primal needs. A human life is not a beating heart but that for which the heart beats. Human life is not just that we live but that we live for something more.

Our bodies are worldly shells, convenient physical cupboards for our supernatural minds and divine souls. A man that lives only to eat, drink, and sleep must seem to be much like a monkey, or a lesser animal even. An animal consumes to survive; a human does more, something that animals cannot, taking advantage of what makes man different than any other life form: mind and soul, intellect and will.

Death results in a permanent break with the natural world: our lifeline is severed. When our minds and souls, eternal parts of ourselves, what departs from our bodies upon death, what Homer called *psyche,* is no longer capable of interacting with the physical world through our bodies, the physical part of ourselves. When we have shuffled off our mortal coils.

## *Subtle death of our human selves.*

The termination of our biological processes, the death we share with animals, is not the only form of death for humans. There is another, more subtle death—the gradual and premature departure of the mind and other human faculties from the physical body.

Our time to self-actualize is slipping away as our abilities degenerate. We might expect to live until age one hundred, but we may only be able to exercise our most human faculties while we are young. By age forty or fifty, our minds may begin to lose sharpness as our joints lose flexibility and we become more prone to sickness.

For example, a man loses his mind to age before his heart stops beating. It is not that he has lost just any capability; it is that he has lost the human faculty of intellect. Especially if the faculty lost was essential to his self-actualization—if, for example, the old man was a brilliant mathematician before having lost his mind.

In some ways we control the degeneration of our abilities by living safe and healthy lives. We might reasonably expect, then, to decrease the rate of this subtle death; however, our fragile bodies are still subjected to unexpected accidents, which we cannot control.

For example, a man suffers a stroke that induces a coma. His heart beats and his lungs breathe while he metabolizes food fed through a tube—he has not ultimately died but seems to have become less than human, unable to survive by his own means, unable to become who he had the potential to be before.

Even if we slow the rate of our degeneration and keep from unnecessary risk to avoid accident, we are still mortal, powerless over many of the conditions of our existence. Therefore, we must consider not only when we are to be buried in the ground, but also, and subtly more urgent, the death of our capable, human selves.

As our minds slow, senses dull and joints creak, we become less able, so we must quickly do that for which we were made, that which distinguishes our species from animal.

Before we give in to lazy pleasures and elderly frailty we must quickly perform in our prime, to self-actualize, so that we might grow old peacefully, having made use of our youth and its abilities.

### The present is all that we control.

Wedged between two sequential moments there exists the present, transcending time itself like an infinitesimal river that cuts ever so thin between the mountains of past and present. We live here, in the river between the mountains.

In the present, who we were in the last moment dies, reborn into the next moment as whoever we become as result of whatever we did in that sliver between past and future.

Each nanosecond is filled with potential: knowledge we can learn, successes we can achieve, opportunities we can take—all at the opportunity cost of whatever else we might do in that very instant.

Death can be managed if we control these present instants, taking advantage of each moment before it passes while constantly thinking of the loss that surrounds us—the instants gone by and all the instants that will inevitably be taken all at once.

### Carpe diem.

It is something difficult to comprehend that I am dying every second, and I am left with an ambiguous amount of motivation to live presently. For whole weeks, even months at a time I will forget that I am finite, caught up in the pleasures of a basic human life.

But then I remember, and begin again to live as if each day is my last, tricking myself into considering very seriously that I will die tomorrow. Not because I want to die, but because death is a great motivator as the subtle thief of the rest of my life.

### A good death.

When I was younger, I never understood the glory of a soldier's death. Now, it seems to me that it is a good death: to die on the battlefield. It is a soldier's nature to be a warrior, his purpose to fight, and therefore his destiny to die in battle.

He trains his body and develops his ability to wield a weapon. He wakes each morning and works until exhaustion to become a greater warrior so that he might triumph when he meets his enemies on the battlefield. He trains to be all that he can.

He fights many battles and defeats many enemies but eventually enters a battle where his army is outnumbered. He must smile then, that this might be the battle worthy of claiming his life.

He meets more than several attackers at once and strains every muscle for all that each has trained, wielding his weapon as a warrior with the skill of many years. He defeats many of them, but even for as great a soldier as he is, as all that he could be, as all that his nature would allow, he is still human, and he is struck down.

This is a good death: fighting to the limit of his well-trained ability before exiting existence self-actualized, pressed up against the limit of all that he could have been.

Our potential is relative to time. If this soldier had survived this battle, he would have returned to camp and trained more to enter into the next battle even greater, pressed up against his limits, again and again, until it kills him, and he might depart from time, eternally as all that his finiteness allowed him to be.

Death is not a curse, but a blessing that frees us from the time-relative obligation of constant work and self-actualization. We need not fear death, except that it might meet us as less than we could have been. We need only find our purpose and let it kill us.

A short life is a blessing. A soldier cries tears of joy as he dies on the battlefield. We must fight the good fight, strive after everything, but not for too long, before we are blest with eternal rest, and go peaceful into that last good night.

## Fear of finiteness.

It is natural, a human thing, to yearn for eternity, find meaning in it, and to fear finiteness and non-existence. I, too, used to be anxious that our natural lives must end, that I would lose my loved ones, and that I myself would eventually slip into nothingness. Then, in my thought, I stumbled upon self-actualization.

We may or may not be finite, may or may not have purpose; but self-actualization positions us optimally to take advantage of any situation that we might meet upon death.

Admittedly not an ultimate solution, self-actualization at least frees the human mind from a fear of finiteness to focus on instructing its body to become all that it can in the time it has to live.

There is no reason to fear our nature. We need not worry that we will die because we are not meant to be immortal, not designed for eternity—a man who lives forever is not human.

If we are finite, we must live finite lives as best we can, pressed up against our limits, constantly more, until we can be no more. If we are matter, we must do with our matter all that we can. We need only fear dying as less than we could have been.

We are like flames at the burning end of a finite wick. The wick burns at a constant rate for the most part, yet the point at which the wick ends and the flame snuffs out is unpredictable.

Any attempts to slow the rate at which the wick burns or to lengthen the wick are futile. We need not have anxiety that someday we will be snuffed out: this is our nature. We need only live knowing that our wicks are finite and presently burning.

We need not fear death, but we must remember that we are presently burning, and if it is our nature to be flames we must burn furiously, fearing only to die as less than we could have been, raging against the coming of night, the dying light, until we are snuffed out.

### Finite human lives as segments of infinity.

They say man and God see time differently. Our perception of time is linear, stretched over a finite distance from a beginning point to an ending point. To see time like God, I imagine, is like rotating that line until one point seems to be all points at once. For man, there was and will be. For God, there only is.

Our finite spaces in time are at least segments of eternity, parts of the whole of infinity. We will exist, always, infinite, in a sense, for once having existed, having held a finite segment of time.

It becomes of utmost importance, then, that we live to self-actualize during our small window of time in which we are capable of affecting who we will forever be, so that each of our shares of eternity might be made as great as possible.

Even if there proved to be no eternal significance for human life, I would remain unconvinced that we are to do nothing, to live drunkenly, a life of selfish pleasure, then die.

We are at least capable of producing for others, whereby we are made eternal as the effects throughout and beyond time caused by what we once were and, in some sense, forever will be.

In a sense, Socrates is still alive, immortalized by his works and legacy, still affecting how we think about the world, changing the course of human history. Socrates has affected millions of minds and the structures of our present societies, even after his body has gone.

We live in the sense that we affect existence, interacting with all else that is considered to be living. We can live forever, or at least until the end of this natural world, this interconnected causal system of which we are now forever inextricably part for once having lived.

Like the effect of a butterfly flapping its wings, what we do during our finite lives, even the small things, dramatically affects the bigger picture, painted by the intricacies of a deterministic nonlinear system, of which we are all part. We become immortal, having existed at one time in one space, having played our part in history.

One might argue that animals and plants have this same power like a butterfly flapping its wings. I suppose this is true but only man has the free will to choose how he will affect existence. Even if animals and plants are part of the causal chain, their effects are certainly determined by genetics and the processes of nature, and therefore can be drawn out of the life equation as constants.

If a rational man considers that it is entirely within his own power to make the choice whether his finite existence become infinitely good or infinitely less so, then he must be inclined to desire self-actualization, to become all that he can in finiteness, in order to become the greatest that he can infinitely be. But even Socrates will one day be forgotten. Those who have been and will be forgotten by this world, how do they matter?

There is, of course, the possibility that we live on in another way, more than our effects and the roles our physical selves played in this natural world, but actually as the intangible parts of ourselves—mind and soul—carrying on after our bodies that remain behind here. However, for the same reason we have neglected to talk about other things about which we are not certain, we will also neglect to talk about whether or not we live on in this way.

*Infinite lives would make self-actualization impossible.*

Given enough time, anything can happen. Given infinite time, everything will happen. If we lived infinite lives, then we might accomplish even less than we do during our finite lifetimes.

Assured of our infiniteness, certain of actualizing ourselves and one day becoming all that we could, lifted out from under the weight of death that limits our existence; I wonder if we'd know what to do, or if we would do anything at all. We might just explode.

With infinite lifetimes, our natures would be set as infinite, as everything, only this does not seem to be much of a nature, certainly not human. To be everything must be just *to be*—this surely must be God, He who said, "I am," who, I imagine, has devised an infinite lifestyle because He is designed for it.

But for a human being designed for finiteness to be cast into infinity, holding things in his mind that he might reasonably do at some point in time, but always saying, "Not now, later, not today." With tomorrow guaranteed he might spend each day doing nothing.

If we lived infinite lives, we needn't worry about philosophy, religion, or much of anything really, because we'd figure it out eventually. We'd get drunk and seek pleasure for a great deal of time until the bounds of infinity pressed upon us everything else that is in the realm of possibility, but they might never press upon us.

Man might never strive for anything, because he would eventually, but *eventually* might never come. Even though he might have otherwise accessed things beyond the limits of possibility that bound our natural lives here where possibility is relative to time, he might not, because he would tell himself that he would eventually.

In infinity, surely man would self-actualize, but then again, maybe not. If an infinite human being exercised his free will under this assumption of inevitability in infinity, lazy and unmotivated by an otherwise foreseeable end, then anything, the happening of which would seem to have been inevitable, might never happen.

I find death to be very useful then, to hold in our minds, contemplating the impending proof of our mortality, urging us to live swiftly. In this way, death is God's great gift to humanity, that we might be forced by time to strive to become all that we can.

*Death as an economic argument against suicide.*

Our fragile mortality makes us capable of opting out of the remainder of our lives; suicide gives us the option of premature departure from life and escape to death.

However, life is scarce and death is guaranteed regardless of the length of our lives; therefore, we must not kill ourselves. Though we are not certain of the conditions of death, we assume it is at least absent of natural life as we experience it here. Death also seems to be infinite because it fills the time that continues after our finite lives.

Uncertainty prevents a rational man—one who acts to maximize his own utility—from deciding to end his natural life prematurely, because the conditions of death are not known.

(1) If man lives the length of his natural life and death is infinitely good, then he gains long life and infinitely good death.

(2) If man lives the length of his natural life and death is infinitely bad, then he gains long life despite infinitely bad death.

(3) If man commits suicide and death is infinitely good, then he sacrifices the remainder of his life to gain an infinitely good death.

(4) If man commits suicide and death is infinitely bad, then he sacrifices the remainder of his life to suffer an infinitely bad death.

In summary: If death is infinite and good, we gain infinitely just the same by either living the lengths of our natural lives or opting out early. If death is infinite and bad, we lose infinitely just the same by either living our natural lives or opting out.

In mathematical terms, death is an infinite term and life is a constant adding finite good of life to infinitely good deaths to make our whole existences slightly more good, or adding finite good to our infinitely bad deaths to make our whole existences slightly less bad.

In math, a constant attached to an infinite term by addition is sometimes regarded as negligible in comparison, forgotten in the shadow of perpetual increase and therefore assumed into the infinite term. However, I argue, contrarily, that this finite good offered by life is more than negligible when added to the infiniteness of death, because life is more than math, but also based on the possibility that in some way finiteness is infinite.

It makes economic sense to live as long as our natures will allow, spending every gifted second of a finite life before an assured infinite death. We should not pay with even a small portion of our finite lifetimes to consume infinite resources guaranteed to us by death regardless of the length of our lives. There is no opportunity cost of a long life but the opportunity cost of suicide is the remainder of one's natural life—such a great thing with so much potential.

One might argue: if death is better than life, then suicide makes sense. But this is not enough that death is preferable to life because, even if death is marginally better than life, an economic actor stands to gain from consuming a marginally less valuable resource at no opportunity cost; in this case, each second of life has no effect on the infinite amount of death that is guaranteed.

Even if death were known to be infinite and good, a rational actor lives the length of his natural life if it offers him the potential for some finite good—love, happiness, beauty, art, music. I use the word *potential* because I know for some life has been only bad.

I have heard stories and read books about those in poor conditions, for whom I imagine it is difficult to see the potential for good, for whom death is a friend offering an escape from this world that has treated them so wretchedly.

I do not pretend to know such horrors. To me, this world has been only kind. But I maintain that those presently experiencing bad must live on for potential good. It is our responsibility to fight against criminals and elements of nature that harm our fellow men, so that they might experience good sooner rather than later.

# GREATER GOOD

*JUSTICE AND LOVE*

For what do we live and for what do we self-actualize, if not for others? If we are aware of this power within ourselves to produce for others, can we reasonably do anything but work for them?

If we are greater producers than consumers, able to supply more than our own demand, then in order to self-actualize we must produce for others, consuming just enough to continue producing, spending just enough time on ourselves to survive.

Your fully actualized self is the greatest gift that you can give to the world. Such a self, as capable as possible, as all that you can be, is the most capable curer of disease, solver of economic turmoil, negotiator of peace, philanthropist, and teacher of wisdom.

As all that we can be, we are able to produce much more goodness in the world than our lesser selves.

## Love demands that we live for others.

If to love is to will the good of another—as was taught to me in Catholic school—what inclines us to fall in love with an individual when we might otherwise fall in love with our whole species?

It seems selfish to restrict our love to one individual who might satisfy our own needs for affection and companionship but simultaneously limit our abilities to produce for others.

Why spend so much time with just one other? Especially when we might otherwise think all day about what is our good and how we might produce a great amount of it for a great number of people, not just one, not just ourselves or our lovers.

It is for this reason, I suppose, that my love for humanity burns stronger in my mind and soul than my love for any individual, which burns only in my chest, in my body, rarely making it past my rib cage to my metaphorical heart, beating only for logic and reason.

## To love others, we must first love ourselves.

When I was young, I fell in love with others often but was disappointed until I began to love myself—only then could I truly love others. It seems to me, that in order to love our species, to provide for their good, we must first love ourselves, willing our own good in order to become capable of willing theirs.

For example, a father that loves his family wills their good, and, like any loving father, is inclined to stay home to coddle his child and show affection to his wife, but he is also the breadwinner and must work to provide for his family.

In order to provide for his family he must become efficient at his work, and thus begins the process of actualization. The beginning of this process requires he spend a great deal of time alone, to know himself, to look through himself as a lens to humanity.

He studies himself as a member of the species, coming to know himself more intimately than he is able to know any other individual, even more than he can know his wife and child.

By this process he learns about what is good for a human, then wills it, thinking to produce ideas about how we might attain it, motivated by his needs for justice and love to exercise his breadwinning abilities. He produces first for himself so that he is able to continue producing, and then for his family as the object of his most immediate obligation, and then for humanity as a whole.

After he and his family have been provided for but before the rest of humanity has been provided for, the question then becomes: when does the father stop producing?

How much greater must a father's love for his family be than his love for the rest of humanity in order for him to bring home only enough food to satisfy the appetites of his family members, while other members of humanity still starve?

*Justice demands that we produce for others.*

A selfish man behaves as the sole actor in his own economy. In a one-man economy, the one actor is simultaneously the one consumer and one producer, demander and supplier. The amount produced is set equal to the one actor's ability to supply and the amount consumed is set equal to the demand of his desires.

In such an economy, surplus and shortage are intolerable. Production and consumption should be equal so that the one actor is satisfied without wasting. His time spent producing is valuated as an opportunity cost of consuming his production.

In reality, however, we are not alone in the economy; our production and consumption need not be matched. We are actors in an economy with many others, for whom we must produce, if we are able, because we are born unequal, and some of what is produced by the advantaged is owed to the disadvantaged, as the disadvantaged cannot produce enough for themselves.

*With great power comes great responsibility.*

The advantaged have a responsibility to the disadvantaged. Those given great advantage in a society must work for the benefit of the less advantaged; those whose abilities are within their control must reduce their needs while continuing to improve their abilities of production from which others will benefit.

Like a man who wins the lottery suddenly possesses the power of wealth and does justice by donating at least a portion to charity. We have won the genetic lottery, born with the abilities of a species so powerful, able to affect matter and the lives of others.

We are advantaged just for being human, with great powers to bend and affect matter—our minds operating our bodies like machines to interact with reality. Like a man with great wealth, our human assets make us immensely capable of positive change, and it seems then to be our responsibility to use our abilities for others.

A man aware of his potential must become obsessed with his work, driven to be all that he can as a great creator of good, utility and happiness for a great many others. He does this as his fully actualized self, doing the work of many men in less time. If it is the potential of each member of mankind to be so great ourselves, having the latent capability for a great amount of production, then with this power must come a great deal of responsibility.

We should seek to produce much and consume little, increasing our abilities and reducing our desires for the greater good of others. We do this in the interest of actualizing our selves, but also in the higher interests of justice and love that join us together.

### Education as an example of power with responsibility.

If the education system has taught us students to function as good citizens of the state and fair actors in the economy, how selfish must we then be to produce only for ourselves, or even our families, when we might otherwise produce for so many in greater need?

Students should learn what is good for society and improve their abilities to bring about that good, not only for themselves, but for others too. Yet it seems so many students have a mind for personal gain, not societal welfare. They have already decided that money is what is good for themselves, neglecting to consider if anything is greater than money, or even what is good for others.

These students are concerned foremost with *curriculum vitae* skills, profitable degrees, and grades high enough to meet the cut-off for the highest paying employer. All in pursuit of what is monetarily good for themselves, as opposed to what is truly good for society.

Does our having been born with natural intellect and accepted to a university funded by taxpayers and alumni give us the right to exorbitant wages? Surely we are entitled to a portion of our wages, but how much? Justice suggests we owe a great deal to others.

### We must produce for others to self-actualize.

As humans, I wonder if we are inherently better producers than consumers. It seems that we were created to be economically efficient, capable of surviving while consuming less than we produce, almost as if we were designed for work.

A powerful man, especially, must find it difficult to enjoy luxuries and things that satisfy only himself, if he is aware that he consumes his own time with so little utility output compared to the utility he might otherwise produce if working for others.

Even if he were a utility monster, one man can only consume so much. He must see no purpose in his consumption other than to sustain his production. He must find it in accord with justice that he spend his time producing for others while consuming little himself.

If we are greater producers than consumers, then, in order to self-actualize, we must produce for others, for the greater good, because, if producing all that we can, we cannot consume all this production on our own. If we are greater producers than consumers, then our supply must exceed our demand.

We are able to produce much and consume little; our surplus can be distributed to those in the economy whose need is greater than their ability to acquire, not as a result of their laziness, but as a result of uncontrollable inability. It is our duty to provide for them.

We *can* live for much more than ourselves; therefore, to be all that we can be, it seems we *must* live for others, seeking to produce for them in order to self-actualize. As much as self-actualization is for ourselves, to be all that we can, we also owe an obligation to others, to produce for them, for the greater good.

# ACKNOWLEDGEMENTS

My thoughts herein were greatly influenced by three works: Napoleon Hill's *Think & Grow Rich*, Marcus Aurelius' *Meditations*, and Abraham Maslow's "Theory of Human Motivation."

www.ingramcontent.com/pod-product-compliance
Lightning Source LLC
Chambersburg PA
CBHW060537030426
42337CB00021B/4301